AS IF I CARED

POEMS AND OTHER PARTS OF A LIFE

DAMIAN GORMAN

With best wishes —

Damian Gorman

© Damian Gorman 2020

ISBN: 978-1-83815-120-1

Published by The Junction

The Junction
- Community Relations and Peace Building -

This publication is supported by The National Lottery through the Arts Council of Northern Ireland. The views expressed do not necessarily reflect those of the Arts Council.

The Junction receives core funding support from the NI Communuty Relations Council.

FOR MY LOVED ONES

(Who know who they are)

Love is a boat
On an open sea
Taking its chances
Honestly.

Contents

Preface

Thank you for lifting this book. I've never made one before. I've made poems and plays and television programmes; I've made verse documentaries and verse plays – but never a whole book. A writer, who's lived as a writer for 35 years, without ever submitting a whole book? If you think that's odd, stick around. I'm just getting started.

Seriously, I'm very grateful the Junction thought to ask me. A book just hadn't been on my agenda; I'd been doing other things. I've given countless readings of my poems, and made programmes with them. But as my son says, if I was hit by a bus, you'd have to take my word for it.

So here is a gathering of my words to survive the bus: "poems and other parts of a life", as it says on the tin. Because I love the contact and intimacy of readings, and because that is what I know, I've tried to reproduce it here. There are 11 sections of writing, each introduced with a bit of "chat"; chat which I hope throws some light on the work, and is readable. Taken together, the introductions amount to the bones of a memoir.

Why is it called "As If I Cared"? Because that's the way I move forward. My writing, my bits of vision, my demeanour – they're all better than me. So I try to be prophetic of whatever bit of good I might do: throw the idea of it somewhere in front of myself, and attempt to grow into it.

I hope that makes sense. Or the book does. Or is enjoyable anyway.

Thanks again,
Damian Gorman
October 2020

Ferns

I want to mention something straight away that I'd rather not mention at all. But to leave it out altogether I'd need to bite down on my tongue too hard. It would also leave an emptiness at the heart of this book. But if you detect a tremor of equivocation in the first pages of it, you are right.

My late father was a fishmonger. He was the most sublime ballroom dancer I have ever seen, on television or in life. And he could make us all contract with fear, our mum included.

I know he had a lot on his mind, including the state of his mind. But he seemed to be a man who believed that if problems appear on the road in front of you, you should flatten them *into* the road. Sometimes your children are problems; sometimes your wife is a problem.

And, of course, there was more to him than that. I feel that if by the end of this book you have no time for him at all, I'll have done something wrong – because *I* do. Indeed when I get together with my remaining brothers and my sister we sometimes ask ourselves did the violence happen at all, or is it just a very bad dream that we had together. But I have evidence, photographic evidence.

On a family holiday to Butlins, Mosney in 1970 we posed for a family photograph. Just before the shutter went down I committed some misdemeanour which merited the back of a heavy hand. The others are smiling in the photo. My head is at an angle, a stunned and quizzical expression on my nine-year-old face.

How many times did it happen? I couldn't tell you. Was it regular? Well it was always a factor, and the fear was constant. It made you contract inside. Nor was it the fabled "odd slap that did me no harm". It was at a level that made mum leave for a long time, and take the younger ones with her. It was at a level where I remember sitting on the bus to school, with a blackening eye, in a blind panic. Wondering how I would explain the state of me to the teachers. And lighting on the idea that I could have "walked into a door". Not knowing, really not having a clue, that that's what everyone says.

I'm not saying to you that I staggered, somehow, out of an utterly blighted childhood. It was *my* childhood; obviously I knew no other. And you can always have craic when you've a handful of brothers and sisters. In the days after the family reunited, after dad had lost his shop and had a breakdown, we could make each other hysterical as we helped mum keep the show on the road. Indeed sometimes the fun could be in response to the threat there was.

There were a number of things dad did talk about when he was in good form. Among these was that his own father (Patrick Gorman, "The Singing Butcher") had been Carl Hardebeck, the peripatetic German music teacher's, first pupil in the North. He also told us, with overwhelming reverence, that an uncle of his had died with the words "the Mass, the Mass, my holy Mass" on his lips.

Terrible and all as it is, we found both things hilarious.

The first because the name "Hardebeck" was a hoot and delight to say; and the second because our great uncle's last words seemed to be the same.

And if we detected the storm clouds gathering inside the house, one of us might pop up and say, "dad, was granda really Carl Hardebeck's *first* pupil?", trying not to catch the treacherous, glittering eye of a sibling. Or, riskier still, I might essay – if things were really bad - "dad, what were your uncle's last words again?" If, in the course of this pious enquiry, I had caught an eye and corpsed, I would have *been* a corpse. Fact.

Another thing that could distract or pacify him was ferns. When we were wee he had a fish shop, as I said, and he dressed the fish trays with ferns. He would be pleased if you brought him some, and they were easy enough to find on the fringes of the town or at the feet of the Mournes. He always needed a lot of ferns. And we brought him a lot of ferns. To this day I think of them as having special powers of healing.

As I got a bit bigger I became affronted by his blows. I was offended as well as hurt by them – offended that one person, even your dad, could do this to another. And I determined 2 things at a young age: that I wanted to be a father, a good father, when I grew up; and that I wanted to use *words* in my life as a force for good - words as real in their impact as violence could be.

You might hold that determination in your mind going through this book - even though I was a very young thing when I made it.

The Giant Basket

My father, officially, "wasn't well"
If anyone asked (his nerves were bad).
And every Friday night
I would stand before my mother at the sink.
She'd wet her comb and, somehow, find a shade.
Beads of water lit on her nylon housecoat.

And because I had more sense than Gerard
I would get the giant basket, and the pound,
To "go to Mrs Bell's and Mr Fay
And see if they've anything put aside today
For Mrs Gorman. Make you sure to say
That it's for Mrs Gorman. Don't be long".

It was a brave step up the Shimna Road
On a winter's evening, black and cold.
But oh how lovely it was to feel
Responsible at the age of ten,
Oh how lovely it was
To carry the giant basket for your own ones.

Slightly damaged peaches, day-old bread,
And sausage rolls which flaked more than they should
Were heaped into my basket. Best of all
Were bruised eclairs and buns from Mrs Bell.

And I'd come home like a little fork-lift truck,
Carrying the giant basket out in front.
My brothers and sister whooped and danced about
And my mother made some tea to warm me up.
Even my father, sullen in his chair,
Would be a little brighter with his share,

And, with a deal of anarchy, we'd make
A meal of Friday's tea, and no mistake.

Home

For a year or two after the family got back together we didn't have a home of our own. For the first part of that time we lived in a caravan on a site called Sunnyholme. For us kids it was fine, at least at the start – roaming the fields with children displaced by the Troubles in Belfast; living in a dwelling with buckets 'X' and 'Y' instead of a toilet; gas mantles and beds that fitted into the wall – what's not to like?

But for mum it was tough, and for dad in his way too. I remember being affected by his preparations for a meeting with an independent councillor from Newcastle Urban District Council. I believe this man was on the housing committee, and he was known to be fond of a drop. My dad, a life-long Pioneer (a Catholic Temperance organisation), had to go about organising half-a-dozen beer for the councillor's visit, for that's how it was done then. It pained him to do it, and he wasn't well at the time.

As the summer turned to autumn and the caravan park emptied, it wasn't so much fun. I started at the grammar school, in September 1972, from Sunnyholme. I'll never forget an early maths class in which Venn diagrams were explained to us. The teacher asked us to put up our hands if we had more than one TV in the house; then again, if we had more than the one car parked outside it. It was embarrassing to be outside the two big circles of the diagram, never mind the gilded intersection at its core.

When we eventually left the caravan we were helped to move by a kindly milkman, Oliver King; and a kindly nun, Sr Gonzaga. Our goods and chattels, such as they were, were heaped on the flatbed of a lorry, along with us. I remember my dad carrying into the cab of the lorry the beautiful patent leather ballroom shoes made for him by his grandfather. He did so with great care.

We were allowed to stay in our new home for only one night. Officially, because it turned out that we had a dog (a beloved Kenwood blend of breeds called Bingo). But our parents suspected Sr Gonzaga's presence "showed what we were".

AS IF I CARED

The next day we moved to a small old bungalow which had a name-plate - "Walton". I remember being heartened by the fact that it bore the name of the TV family I idealised and idolised. I thought we'd be there for a long time, but we weren't.

We moved to a flat above a grocery shop in Railway Street. The building was right beside the covered market, which our mum clothed us from, to dad's embarrassment and anger. But by now she was working in a cafe and cleaning people's houses and, being the only one of them working, had more of a say in where to spend her own money. One day she bought me a market version of the Starsky and Hutch cardigan all the rage at the time. I was sure it would cover my fatness like a magic blanket, and make me attractive. But the garment was so thin you could have spat through it, and I looked more like a Mr Man hemmed in by a belted dishcloth.

But that was a good summer, the summer of 1973. We were roaming around again in company, and the music was good – *Life on Mars, You Can Do Magic, Stuck in the Middle With You, Dancin' on a Saturday Night* ... Again I thought we'd be *there* for a good while, but we weren't.

As the summer drew to a close our house was bombed. Which is to say that the grocery shop below us was bombed. It was owned by a man said to be a former B-Special, and we were led out into the night, a wee while before the device exploded, in great fear and excitement. Even at a safe distance, it was by far the loudest noise I'd ever heard. I've been completely deaf in my left ear since I was a baby. For the whole night after the explosion I was deaf in both.

This time we moved to a home: a rented house on a new council estate, but a home of our own – 5 Mourne Rise. The house we were allocated was the exact one that dad had placed a miraculous medal in the foundations of many months before. As true as I'm sitting here. And if you don't believe me, ask Gerard, Declan or Moya.

And this 3-bedroomed house was where the 7 of us settled. All the bouncing around of the previous period has left me with a horror of "flitting", as moving house is called in Northern Ireland. And an empathy, a real fellow-feeling, for anyone who's had to leave their homeplace, anywhere in the world.

Available Light

(Commissioned by the Irish International Immigrant Centre,
now the Rian Immigrant Centre, Boston)

When we reach the world we're taken by the hand
Or into the hands of someone, someone kind,
A midwife maybe – someone who knows our worth
Is more than the weight we put upon the earth,
Who knows that the very hollows of our bones
Are filled with light, with grace, the secret flames
That we arrive with when we reach this place
And which, if they're unfurled, can cure the darkness.

So when we move around the world we're more
Than "wretched refuse of a teeming shore"
We're light – all the available light there is.
And, if we meet each other at our borders
And turn each other down, then something dims
Right there, and everywhere: the darkness wins.

Tá fáilte romhaibh

(Facebook post, written on August 28, 2015,
in response to the finding of bodies in an abandoned lorry)

If life, decent life, is not possible where you are, you have the right to move anywhere you might find it – anywhere in the world – and that includes the house attached to my house, in my part of the world.

And it's not even a right. It's *in* you, this particular urge. Like the stretch that's inside bones; like the workings of the heart and lungs.

And I know that life should be viable where you start out. Yes it should, and that's a big issue we should speak, and do other things about. But life is not always viable where you start out. And, rather than welcome people fleeing from unbearable want, we erect walls and put people standing in the gated gaps of them to say – on our behalf - "you have no business here".

And what is the result? The result is a dreadful soup of humanity in an abandoned lorry on the Austro-Hungarian border; an awful stew, that might contain 20 people or 50 people, but actually 71 people. The result is bodies littering the waters of the Mediterranean like the discarded wrappings of *things*.

And still the walls go up. And still we employ people to say for us, "you have no business here, in this place, among us". Well my point – my only point – is this: that there is no clear, no necessarily-big difference between saying to desperate people, "you have no business here, among us" and "you have no business here, in this world".

Let people come. *Agus tá fáilte romhaibh*, as we say in Irish. And you are welcome.

Other People's Views

(Facebook post from September 1, 2017)

Just below where I live is a track by the Dyfi river. I walk it twice a day with my labrador, Thomas. He's old now and isn't well, but every evening, round about 7, he gathers himself from his bed and comes looking for me. He drops a ball at my feet and tries to flip me out of my chair with a muzzly heft. It's a moment he insists on every evening. And so do I.

We walk to a gate at a turning on the track, where we stop. It's estuary country here, and the landscape and light are very particular. About 7pm, at this time of the year, the last of the sun going down behind Pennal glances off the water nearest me turning it spangly and golden. Last night it was like Lucozade; like the first pressing of the finest Lucozade ever.

I love this view across this stretch of water. I take my whole self to it, not just my eyes. And though I am not Welsh, I consider it mine.

And my simple point here is just that that's fair enough – that your heart is entitled to "own" the landscape it goes out to. Whoever you are. Wherever you started out.

Party Pieces

I don't remember dad hitting mum in Mourne Rise. Though for the rest of us the fear was still palpable – as was the sense of being able to exhale when he wasn't there.

Every Friday night he went out to play poker or bridge. He was a very good bridge player, and one of the disappointments I brought him was an inability to retain even the rudiments of the game (despite being the one at "The Red High").

When the cat was away, the mice used to have wee concerts. For a long run of Friday nights the rest of us would be joined by Marie, a young woman whose parents mum used to work for, and who herself was very kind to us all; and Michael, a kind English teacher who played the guitar and was losing his hair.

We all had party pieces. Mum's varied between recitations like *Ireland's Queen* or *My Dear Little 55* and romantic ballads such as *Just a Little Love, a Little Kiss* and *Put Your Sweet Lips a Little Closer to the Phone*. My two youngest brothers used to smash it with their full-concert, a cappella version of *Bohemian Rhapsody*, and Michael wowed us every week with Ralph McTell's *Streets of London*.

I loved those evenings, we all did, because they were safe. They were safe havens of good-natured fun; evenings when you could expand rather than contract. And I remember hoping that they would never, ever end.

People politely tholed my own contributions – eclectic offerings of Irish language poems and bodhran solos. And then, just around the time when some of the company were finding better things to do on a Friday evening, I started to introduce a poem or two of my own. (To my genuine horror my brother Gerard remembers the words of *Johnny*, one of my earliest public efforts, about a little blind boy who, in many respects, could see better than any of us...)

Though never on the bill at these ceilidh evenings, dad had a clutch of party pieces of his own. These included a funny version of *Cannons to the Right of Them* and the comic songs *The Little Shirt Me Mother Made For Me* and his own bespoke version of *Galway Bay*. These were usually delivered in outside company – *Galway Bay* being tailored to whatever the gathering was, and whoever was in it.

But his most memorable party piece was one that has me perplexed to this day.

Whenever it could be afforded, the family used to go for a few days in summer to a large guest house in the west of Ireland. The children would be down in the breakfast room, ravenous with hunger, as soon as it opened. Mum would come a bit later; and dad later still, once breakfast was in full swing. And one morning each trip (we'd never know which) he would arrive into the crowded room like a liner among small boats – a tall-ish man in the full regalia of a woman. He would greet people at other tables, lavishly and by name, and would eventually dock at our own table, where we would all be burning with embarrassment.

Now what was that about? The thing is, while he was tall-ish, mum was emphatically not. So he must have had to source his own skirts, bras and God knows what for these occasional performances.

The fact is, of course, that it's none of my nosey business. But in what *is* my business nowadays I am (thank God) regularly asked to say a number of pieces of my own. Here are 3 of my most-requested ones, my party pieces if you like: an attempt (in a play) to write a row between a couple in real time; part of the text of a verse documentary about the Troubles that I made for BBC2; and a poem I was commissioned to write for the Poetry Jukebox to mark 20 years since the signing of the Good Friday Agreement.

Best of order please ...

Martin and Claire

(Taken from the play The Man in the Moon. The couple are unpacking in their weekend caravan retreat. But all is not well with Martin. It rarely is…)

MARTIN
… Did you remember to check the cooker before we left?

CLAIRE
What did you say?

MARTIN
Did you remember to turn the cooker off after tea?

Claire stops what she's doing.

CLAIRE
Why are you asking me that?

MARTIN
I was only wondering. Well, did you?

CLAIRE
I think I did, yeah.

MARTIN
You *think* you did?

CLAIRE
Well I didn't, you know, stand in front of the thing and take a mental Polaroid and say to myself, "I've done that now. I'm sure that's done. Now I can go off and enjoy my weekend"!

MARTIN

But you're sure that it's off?

CLAIRE

I *think* that it's off.

MARTIN

(*Grumbles, as he turns to root in his tape box*)
I was only wondering...

CLAIRE

No you weren't Martin, you were only *worrying*. You're like a friggin patent worry dispenser – one anxiety's taken away, and another falls down to fill the space.

MARTIN

Aw shit.

CLAIRE

What's the problem now?

MARTIN

I've left half of my bloody tapes at home. There's only two of my going-away tapes here. Aw *shit*!

Beat.

CLAIRE

Martin, I know this is tough on you now. You've forgotten some tapes, some special tapes, but you've still got me and the kids – that should count for something.

MARTIN

Oh you're very bloody funny.

CLAIRE

Well what am I supposed to do – sit down and weep?

MARTIN
You're *supposed* to allow me to say "aw shit", and leave it at that.

CLAIRE
And leave it turning round in the air?

MARTIN
That's right.

CLAIRE
In all its gem-like splendour?

MARTIN
That's bloody right!

A moment or two of silence, during which they resume unpacking. Martin speaks first.

MARTIN
Look I don't want to fight on our holiday.

CLAIRE
Well don't then!

MARTIN
But you've got to let me say how I feel, and you must let me *feel* it.

CLAIRE *(Word by slow word)*
I was making a joke – I was trying to lighten you up.

MARTIN
I know I know, and I over-reacted. I'm … *(half-swallows the word)* …sorry.

Beat. She relents.

CLAIRE
So who did you leave behind?

MARTIN
Aretha and Bowie

CLAIRE
Sure they can mind the house when the kids are at their gran's.

MARTIN (*Bit miffed at it being taken so lightly*)
I am annoyed you know Claire.

CLAIRE
Oh I do Martin, I do know that.

MARTIN
It seems such an insignificant thing to you, but it's important to me. We don't get away very often, and when we do it's only for 2 or 3 days. And to tell you the truth, it's like work to me.

CLAIRE (*Incredulous*)
Being on holiday?

MARTIN
Being on holiday, yes.

CLAIRE
Oh Martin, give me a break. Give yourself a break. Give us both a break for 48 bloody hours.

MARTIN
I am trying to explain to you that it takes me time to relax into the holiday, to *exhale*. And by the time I've done that we're thinking about getting packed up and heading for home. But -

CLAIRE
Martin!

MARTIN

But Claire, the point is I made up those special tapes to shorten the decompression time, if you like. I made them up for the pair of us, not myself. This is the music that makes the world right for me – that makes it friendly, wholesome, wonderful. So it helps me into the holiday, and it helps me enjoy the … whaddayyacallit … *(floundering a little)* … the sea, and the … beach – and all the other things. And I *am* sorry that I've left half of that behind – probably the best, most evocative half. And so should you be.

CLAIRE

Oh I am … but I wish you could hear yourself. We're two minutes into our holiday, and discussing what a trial enjoyment is for you. It's a difficult thing, it's a burden, and it is work to have two days off by the seaside with your wife. And you carry this weight like an ant with an outsize load; you carry this cross like Jesus Christ himself. And I am supposed to wipe your face with my dress, and pour myself like ointment over your wounds. Well *fuck-that-Martin!*

MARTIN *(Aghast)*
What?

CLAIRE

I'm not finished yet. You have left your Aretha Franklin tape at home. Well that is a *fact*, it's not a creeping illness. It's something you can turn your back on – I'm sorry, it's not. It's something that any *sane* person could turn their back on. But you never turn your back on a worry, do you Martin? They bring out the Mother Teresa in you – you take them in, you feed them up, you keep them alive as long as you possibly can.

MARTIN
I'm not listening to this.

CLAIRE
I know, you should put on your music. That'll sweeten the moment for you. That'll make it all right.

Beat.

MARTIN *(With grave deliberation)*
This has gone from ... discussion ... into an all-out personal attack on me ... into cruelty.

CLAIRE
Well thank you for plotting that out. It has *gone* too far. And it's gone on for far too long, and it has to stop. I know you like music, I know it means a lot to you; but I don't think you know what it means – it's a jamming device. It's supposed to keep out all the noises you don't want to hear.

MARTIN
Is that what it is?

CLAIRE
Yes it is, and it drives me crazy. And I'll tell you something else – you can't feel good without it. You can't come here and stare at the water, or look at the moon, or talk to *me*, without an accompanying soundtrack enhancing your feelings. And *that's* serious Martin; that's a problem.

MARTIN
Well thank you for it. I collect them you know. It's kind of a hobby of mine.

Beat. Then Claire holds up her hands in "surrender".

CLAIRE
I'll see you later.

MARTIN
Where are you going?

CLAIRE
I'm going out to have a look at the moon. Do you remember the moon Martin? It's the thing in *Moondance, Blue Moon, Moon* – feckin – *River*!

Exits.

From
Devices of
Detachment

I was born in 1961
When things were quieter than they had been:
An IRA campaign had petered out -
They could arouse no interest in the fight.

And at home, between the mountains and the sea,
My father's shop was ticking over nicely.
And people seemed to mix well in the town.
It was a quiet time, the gloves were on.

And the dramas that I heard of as I played,
The stories that were told above my head,
Were not, at first, of bigotry and blood.
There was a coalman who had disappeared,
Without an indication or a word,
His car abandoned on a harbour road -
It was like something out of Hollywood.
But when the movies really came to town,
It was like nothing we had ever seen.

And the decent people I was reared among
Deplored, of course, the Troubles "carry on".
And spent the early evenings sitting near
The television news, as if it were
A kind of posting, or a source of heat.
We seemed to draw some comfort from the thought
That, if the fighting men were on the screen,
It somehow closed around them, like a tin.
If rioting and death were on the news,
Sure it kept them off the streets and avenues.

But sitting still, as we did, was a form
Of waiting for our turn to come. It came.

And we are so weary now. We're like
Exhausted people home from work
Who want to eat, who want to drowse
Beside the television news.
And we have watched – for 40 years -
Across the trays upon our knees,
Repeated warnings, we ignore
That the house is burning down next door.
But it's not ours, so we can sit
Within our chairs, and sleep on it;
It's not ours, so we can sit
Within our chairs, and sleep on it.

Except
That the space a person occupies is huge,
And murdered people do not go away
Like bins collected on a Wednesday
And emptied far away from us, somewhere.
What's nourished by our silences lives here
In graves, the cold rooms of forgotten things;
In these, the warehouses of our sufferings.

It is a tribute often paid to us
That we have coped with everything that's come.
But we have coped too well – the heart is numb -
And other people's sorrow falls like rain
Upon a window or a second skin
That's grown across the mouth and eyes and ears,
And has been called "resilience" down the years.

But what are we – no, what am *I* – to do?
Did I not try to march a mile with you?
For what seems like a summer in my teens
We did not opt for nightmares over dreams.
The marches gave us hope, and let us sing.
We felt we could walk through the Troubles then.
But after rallies we would stand and wait,
Like hungry people at a garden fete.
We wanted peace upon a paper plate;
We wanted someone else to dish it out.

And I felt that peace could come here like a song
That carried all before it. I was wrong.
There's so much pain that can't be sung away,
That goes untreated, that is even stored
As if it were an heirloom, or reward.
We hold it in our hearts, we guard it well:
It is the hidden treasure of my people -
The wealth of suffering that we have met,
And it is time that we let go of it.

Which is much easier to say than do,
For the dead, and what they did, are dear to you.
But we will incubate within our graves
The virus that has torn so many lives
If we don't lay our sense of hurt to rest,
If we do not attend the living first.

I've come to point the finger,
I'm rounding on my own -
The cagey, decent people I
Would count myself among.
Who are like boats at bay,
Like eggs inside their shells,

Like torches without batteries,
We are like covered wells.
We are like rows of idle hands,
We are like lost or mislaid plans,
We are like tears that do not fall -
We are no fuckin use at all.

And in the end it all comes down to this:
The North of Ireland is a tiny place.
And if someone's killed – and I don't care by who -
The whole thing happens right in front of you.
To step around it is a choice that's made:
We take the scenic route among the dead.
And I speak about these things to save my life,
For I have slowly come to understand
That, just as surely as the sea takes land,
The Ulster Troubles could absorb *my* death

And there are very few would pause for breath.

If I was us, I wouldn't start from here

Especially in a broken home like ours,
Where broken floors and windows feed the cold,
Each generation has a sacred task:
To tell a better story than it was told.

For we are reared by stories in such places,
Clawing through the bitter draughts of these
For something we can truly get a hold of
That seems to help us off our shattered knees.

The kind of myth my generation supped
Was, "we have better heroes than they've got.
For ours are much more decent – to a fault.
And, if we've a rotten apple, they've the rot".

Our steps now are, at best, precise and formal
Like dressage horses going nowhere well.
Our peace a thing we part-baked in the 90s
And left to prove, and got used to the smell.

Yet even in this half-peace we are living
Where death is only half-dead, I am sure
That we could learn to change our tunes completely,
But if I was us, I wouldn't start from here.

If I was us I wouldn't start from here
For Here's a swamp we've stood in for too long.
We haven't kept our heads above the water,
And haven't seen a thing where we have gone

And we should fly now – frightened for our children -
Kick off the bottom; rush towards the air;
And break the water into different daylight
And gasp; and say what we can see from there.

For especially in a broken home like ours,
Where broken floors and windows feed the cold,
Each generation has a sacred task:
To tell a better story than it was told,

A story made, as honey is in bees,
From things that we have found outside ourselves.

Aw now, houl on

In my teens I hadn't much of a clue about sex. And the clues that I had were misleading, or just plain wrong. I knew that I much preferred the company of girls, even though I was briefly in a band with my mates ("Pagan", the wild men of South Down rock), and really enjoyed that. I longed for the company of girls rather than fellas but, being in a single-sex school, had no real idea how to access it.

For a period that didn't seem to matter, as I was going to be a priest. I went on the odd retreat for young fellas thinking in this direction, but it soon became clear to the vocations director, and then to me, that I hadn't whatever it took. I hadn't it in spades. And if I'm honest, I kept the idea that I might be a priest alive beyond its time, because of my dad. It lowered the threat level for me – perhaps one of God's anointed in its chrysalis. He even told me once that he would "scrub floors to send me to Maynooth".

It was good while it lasted.

The thing about preferring the company of women has lasted to this day. But, as I said, back then I hadn't a clue how to speak to women. Or, more accurately, I hadn't a clue how to cross the distances - the seemingly-vast distances between me and them - to get into talking range. And I was looking for clues. I used to listen to the bigger boys in our school smoking hut in the hope that a clue or two might drop to the floor from their lips. They never did. And it was worse than that.

One day one of the bigger boys said to me, "well Gorman, I saw you talking to Majella after Mass on Sunday". (And indeed I had been talking to Majella. I was giving her a message for her dad about a fish order from mine.) I smiled a manly acknowledgement that yes, I had been talking to an actual girl. "And ...?", continued the big lad, "did you get anything?"

The truth is I didn't know what there was to be got. Which was unfortunate, as the smoke room grew silent, hands clasping reeking fags were stilled, and all eyes were on me: "Aye Gorman, what did you get?"

I mean what was one supposed to get outside half-eleven Mass? But I had to say something, and I said, or whimpered, after an age: "oh you know, eh, just ...the usual".

The place erupted in joyous hacking coughs.

A year or two later, outside the Wilmar bar – head swirling with Galliano, notions, and uncertainty - I found myself up against a wall with an older woman. Kissing I knew about (I had practised this on my own), but not what happened next. She put a warm hand down my trousers but, warm and all as it was, I was out of my depth.

"Aw now," I said, "houl on..."

This mixture of appetite, ignorance and timidity – of wanting to "make love", but not quite knowing the ingredients – was with me for a good (or bad) while. There are traces of it in this wee section – starting with the first poem I ever had published (outside of the school magazine, *Squawk*). Then continuing with a section from my chapter of the *Great Journeys* book accompanying the BBC series of the same name, and finishing with a bit of craic I wrote for Radio 3. (If you've read so far, you might recognise a thing or two there.)

The
Stone

I lifted a stone
And in the naked soil there danced a beetle,
Epileptic.

And I'm fearful of how I would be
If someone should lift that stone
From me.

From
Great Journeys

(In the footsteps of Hernan Cortes in Mexico)

I was ready to leave Veracruz and begin my journey inland to Mexico City. I had just joined the crew in the *zocalo* **for some late night refreshment, when this woman walked up to our table out of nowhere.**

"Why are you wearing the same shirt for 3 days now?", she asked me very evenly, and I was flattered – flattered that she should notice this thing about me. I explained, a little grandly, that it was to do with continuity and so on ... She said that she'd like to talk to me, and asked if I'd go for a walk with her somewhere. In my pale heart a committee of old men deliberated. "*Talk*, what does she mean by talk. And as for a *walk* ..."

But I knew that if I was to be frightened of walking and talking, I might as well give up on this and every other journey. So I went with the woman, I walked with her to the seafront. And she gave me a beautiful present – a piece of her story. She told me about her life in Veracruz; her hopes for her 2 young children and herself. She told me about the dreams she has of her dead child – dreams in which the youngster takes her by the hand across a lovely quiet sandy place, where only the child leaves footprints, for that is *his* world. She told me about the new life she hopes for in Canada, and how she occasionally will leave the kids with her mother, and walk around Veracruz just looking for someone to talk to.

There was much much more, but I cannot reproduce the humour and the frankness of her talk. But underneath the sky in Veracruz, in an open-handed undemanding way, a person gave me a little piece of her heart. And that isn't something that happens every day. Her name was Martha, and in opening up to me she made me feel welcome, even special, in her country. I felt myself starting to fall in love with it then. And I'd nearly missed out on that by being stupid, being awkward and reticent to the point of crudeness. I was so relieved that I'd found a spoonful of courage – the courage to walk and talk in Veracruz.

From
Minty Walsh – Liner Notes
for the 3rd Album

(A fictitious musical memoir)

In November 1999, when Rathlin Records released "Minty" Walsh's *The Humours of Loughareema*, Pipers and Piping magazine announced the arrival of "a new uileann piper for a new millennium". Two years later *Safe Home* confirmed "Minty" as the leading piper of his generation – the Irish Times commenting simply that, "the man has found his instrument, and the instrument has found its man".

But there was more truth – more raggedy, poignant truth in the heart of that remark than the reviewer perhaps realised – because for many years "Minty's" search for an instrument that would be the making of him, the saving of him, that would "release him into himself as an artist" was indiscriminate and frustrating. As he has put it himself, "I was a kind of musical alcoholic – trying everything: lifting it, downing it; being satisfied by nothing."

Small wonder, then, that he became a straightforward alcoholic too.

But now, with the release of *The Wide World Over*, "Minty" Walsh has left dissatisfaction – and drink – far behind him. Produced by the American folk-fusion legends Woody Walls and Steve Ding, this record will bring new audiences flocking to him, like the unfettered waves of his beloved Irish Sea. His collaborations with the likes of Stormzy and Philomena Begley have to be heard to be believed.

A good time, then, to reflect on the life of the man.

Gerard Majella Walsh was born on the 27th of August 1962, on a caravan site outside Newcastle County Down, Northern Ireland. His mother and father both had summer engagements in this resort town – Eileen as drummer with the Cauled Cap Ceilidh Band, and Martin as *"Marty Walsh – the Singing Plasterer"*. Growing up in such a musical environment it was, perhaps, inevitable that the young Gerard

Majella would turn his hand, or have it turned, to the family business; and just as inevitable that his first instrument would be the tin whistle. Studious, technically-gifted, and blond, Gerard was playing Kerry polkas for grim relatives – and a paying public – by the age of 3. Had it not been for recurrent bouts of childhood asthma and head lice, he may well have delighted those audiences into his teens. As it was he gave up music for a number of years, preferring schoolwork and shuttle diplomacy between his parents.

When his parents separated, or *were* separated in 1976, Gerard shaved his fashionably-full head of hair entirely. This was partly in protest at the separation, and partly an attempt to be rid of head lice once and for all. And it was at this baldy time that he received the nickname for which he is known the uileann piping world over.

Various legends have arisen as to the origin of that nickname, but the truth – as I have it from the man himself – is heart-warmingly banal. Unaware that he was using a eucalyptus-based shaving foam on his head, a girlfriend told Gerard – in the hearing of others – that his ears smelled like mint. Out of such rough, even poor, material are the soubriquets of genius made.

But back in the dark days of the mid-to-late 70s genius was the last thing on Gerard or "Minty's" mind. The separation of his parents had wounded him deeply, and for a time he sought consolation – as so many have done - in after-school clubs. But the Debating Society could only help up to a point, and "Minty" has since recalled this time as the first of several major crossroads in his life. "I could have gone either way," he has said, "I could have turned in on myself, or come out as a rebel".

In the event, thanks to the magic of music, he was able to do both – for in 1978 he resumed his musical career, becoming bass player with introspective punk band *Mis-spent Fiver*. Sustained by a small but devoted following of South Down nihilists, *Mis-spent Fiver* gigged fitfully until the autumn of 1979 when musical differences, or *in*differences, saw their project parked in limbo. "I don't know why," says "Minty", "but all the joy had gone out of it somehow. It was a blow when we split up, but I'd mastered the bass guitar, so I was coming out ahead. And – as I kept telling myself – nobody had died".

In 1980 his father, reluctantly, did die. Unhinged by not being able to see it, his mother Eileen joined a sect in Donegal which, among other things, empowered her to become childless again, and – cut off from even her wayward ministrations - "Minty" took to the drink. He gave himself over to it completely. He swam in it, open-mouthed, as if he were swimming in his beloved Irish Sea.

In fact, of course, "Minty" was sinking – sinking fast. In despair he flung out an arm, and what did it find? The raft that is music, his salvation – he found a clarinet. And for 3 years – most of his time as a student – he kept body and soul together as clarinettist with experimental jazz-rock combo *Duplex*. "It was cool white music at a black, black time," he told me. "It was therapy, a kind of crossword, and it paid the bills. I could do it asleep or drunk. And I often did."

It was at a series of *Duplex* gigs in 1983 that "Minty" fell in love with, and later met, the actress and singer Assumpta-Mary Brownfoot. She was everything that he was not – confident, worldly-wise, talentless – and he loved her not only for those qualities, but also for her looks. She was a stunningly beautiful woman, and very tall. She was also responsible for at least a partial reconciliation between "Minty" and Eileen, who began to speak to her son again, and attempted to legally adopt his girlfriend.

In a rush of love "Minty" gave up the *Duplex* gig, taught himself the concertina, and became Assumpta-Mary's manager and accompanist. For her part, she became heavily pregnant, and was able to stop singing. It was an arrangement which suited her audiences.

With the births of Cuchulainn and Ferdia in 1985 "Minty" embarked on the happiest, most unproductive years of his life. Drawing the dole, and doing just a little cash-in-hand session work, he was able to take his young family swimming 3 mornings a week. He was also free to take them for extended visits to his mother's home in the Donegal Gaeltacht, but chose not to do so. He cut his drinking and manic depression to acceptable levels, and taught himself bassoon and viola, to amuse the twins.

Life was good, life was sweet, and it was stretched out before him – sparkling, like his beloved Irish Sea.

But round about 1990 Assumpta-Mary and the boys started wanting things other than swimming – the sorts of things that only money can buy – and "Minty" was forced into learning, and teaching, the piano. In his own socially-awkward way he had a gift for teaching and, financially, the move into the world of regular work was a success. In every other respect, however, it came crashing around him.

And the name of that crash was *Siobhan* – spelt properly, with no 'v'.

"Minty's" classes attracted pupils of all ages and heights, and he charged £4 an hour (inclusive of incidental photocopying). Siobhan Green, one of the Greens of *Green Meats*, was more then able to pay. She was a beautiful woman, as tall as she was red-haired, and was the first person to ever tell "Minty" that he had lovely hands. Before long their fortnightly sessions became weekly, then twice-weekly. But no one suspected anything untoward at all – least of all "Minty", who was quietly pleased with the woman's application.

Siobhan suggested that they have the lessons in her house as her husband was dead – ensuring that they wouldn't be disturbed in their time together. "Minty" agreed with polite enthusiasm. He was impressed by her home. He was intrigued by the fact that she seemed to have no piano.

The emergence of an affair was a shock to "Minty" and Assumpta-Mary both. Neither of them had seen it coming, and neither knew what to do. "Minty" attempted to win his wife back with the harpsichord, but his efforts were in vain. She said that she would neither love him nor leave him; that he had to stop teaching; and that she would never swim with him again as long as she lived.

She was true to her word. She would sit in the spectators' gallery glaring down at the water, like a baleful moon or Vesuvius above Pompeii. "Minty" and the boys would smile and wave up at her ... at their peril.

In the end he hitched his employment star to the line-dancing epidemic that was sweeping Northern Ireland at the time, and secured a residency in *The High Chaparral* outside Ballymena. They say it takes a worried man to sing a worried song, so "Minty's" foray into country music was unsurprising. He sang from the heart and soul of a great sadness, and the crowd roared their enjoyment. Especially the older people, who remembered his father, *The Singing Plasterer*.

"What are you the Singing?", somebody asked him one night. When the question was explained to him, "Minty" gave a rueful smile. "Oh me? I'm The Singing *Wound*," he joked. It might have been a joke, but he wasn't very happy.

He was, however, a success – at least in North Antrim. The Chaparral crowds grew bigger and older, because of him. And he was good – good enough to give them what they wanted. He always ended each set with his stunning cover of *Walk Backwards When You Leave Me Darlin', So I'll Think You're Coming In*. And it always brought the house down.

By the neck

The things I wrestled with as a young man were not unique. There was a cocktail of fear, wanting, lack of confidence about many things, and having no real idea of how big the horizon could be. So what? I was a very young man.

But I was a very young *Northern Irish* man at a particular time. A time when the Troubles were always there, or thereabouts. Even if they weren't always on the main stage you knew, for a fact, that they were somewhere in the wings. And in that atmosphere some of us developed a talent for unhappiness.

But not to drag things down too far, let me say that I made a discovery which seemed to help me with my "issues": alcohol. If my various ticks and vulnerabilities were boats, this was the very stuff that appeared able to rush into the harbour and raise them from their mud. It allowed me to speak to women with a degree of apparent confidence (and to try my own hand at a few other things foreby).

One thing that alcohol didn't help with was dad. His reaction to you coming in late with the smell of drink on you was straightforward – you were put out. My 3 brothers and I slept in the one room, and whoever was in would decant any late arrivals through a small window in our bedroom, until that ruse was stymied. I was put out many times, and spent many a night in the promenade shelters or elsewhere. Fine (-ish) in the summer; less so when you could watch the ice forming. My brother Brendan was often put out for weeks at a time.

And sometimes that wave which raised my boats was so strong that it carried them right out into the open sea. More about that later, but when I went to college in Belfast I drank every penny I had, and whatever pennies you would part with. I ended up in many tight and strange situations, including drinking in a UDA pub when nowhere else was open, and tapping money from strangers for the bus home when Belfast was sick of me.

But on a more positive note, I fell in love with a married woman. I was 19, she wasn't; she was a mature student, I wasn't; she was gorgeous and thoughtful … well you get the point. So much was happening it was like I was living in a film. Big stuff: having an affair with a married woman. And dreaming – against every odd there's ever been – about a life with her, even a secret one.

Until one day, when I was sitting with her at lunchtime in the upstairs bar of the Student Union, the *Speakeasy*. I had a bottle of Tuborg Gold, by the neck, in front of me. She was upset, and I was doing my limited best to be helpful, when an arm appeared over my right shoulder, out of the blue.

It was a man's arm, and a man's hand caressed the neck of the bottle in front of me. "Is this him?" said a man's voice, a deep voice, with no hint of "give" in it. While his wife tried to reason with him I was rooted to my seat – three-quarters of me paralysed with fear, and the one quarter thinking she shouldn't be left on her own with him. But she told me herself that that was exactly what should happen, and I left as slowly as I felt that the film demanded.

Not once had I seen the man's face. I went into the downstairs loos and put my head under a tap. I'd been sure, in the *Speakeasy*, that the bottle would be broken on my head. My scalp had been alive with preparation for the blow.

What to do about fear, what to do about physical threat, has been a question in my life. As has been, what to do about whatever dreams you retain. In the end I would ask these questions properly – taking them into my poetry, and other places. I would look at how some people have met the darkness with light in the world – by their courage, or by putting a hard edge on their fear. I would get a hold on these things, eventually. When I was fit.

A Coward
at Thermopylae

When we got the word to stand and fight
Till our blood had dried and all was silent,
I nipped out for a doctor's note.
For I hadn't been sleeping well, my eyes were drawn,
And I thought I had a migraine coming on.

I got a chit to leave our hilly fort
And walked away – unpunctured, in disgrace -
To listen, shy, as bone inflected steel:

A war correspondent, with a taste for verse,
Who wanted proof that he might
Be something worse.

Ceathrú

(Ceathrú is the Irish word for a quarter.
It also stood for a quarter acre, at one time thought
to be the smallest holding on which life was viable)

There's a place where we think we can hold out
Against all comers. And by God they come:
Guilt, which like a barrister or panther
Stalks us to the cold edge of the water
Knowing that we can't swim; then there is grief,
When, robbed of you, I'm robbed too of my breath
And, like when we've made love, I gasp your name
As an entreaty, or a benediction.

But there is a place, in the shade, where love abides,
And lives its life in secret, like a heart;
A place which feeds us both – despite its size -
A *ceathrú acra*, quarter-acre plot.
Our souls live there, and will do when we go,
Even if we're the only ones to know.

Human Threads

(For the arpilleristas of Chile, who sewed their truths into
rough cloth, at a time when all truth-telling was banned)

When people lose the thread of being human,
When anything can be done, and often is,
When Power is in its element – which is fire -
And loved ones disappear like scattered ashes,

When Fear and Hatred, in their darkling moment,
Are so full of themselves they blot the sun,
And if you don't want to meet the dark with Darkness
In days, in times like these, what can be done?

Well *arpilleristas* took matters into their own hands,
And charged the fingers of those hands to fight
With needles and with threads and coloured fabric,
And all the blood of their affronted hearts,

To let the love and rage that pulsed within them
And all the scalded grief come to a point.
They warmed that needle-point with what was in them,
They held it till it knew them inside-out,

Then went to work – to stitch Truth into fabric;
To stand before the makers of the Pain
And say, "those loved ones you have taken from us?
We thread them to our torn lives once again.

"Look here they are – for all the world to see -
On this rough cloth, on these white squares of cotton.
And all those crimes you say did not occur
Are stitched here too, and will not be forgotten."

These calls, these protests, special gifts of feeling
Of love, resilience, anger and of strife,
Speak to us with more than words' mere breathing.
They pierce the heart, so it may come to life.

Rumours

There are rumours of things which survive Hell,
But they are only rumours.
Most things – most people – don't,
And that's a fact.

There are rumours of Love being heard above the furnaces:
Glimpsed by the ear as a clearly-separate note
Different from all the roaring going on,
But these are only rumours -
Which says it all.

For rumours are only whispers, which is next to nothing
Like the sound of a kiss, without the kiss itself.
I am tempted to say that, when all is said and done,
The only thing that stacks up is our corpses.

Except that the thing which survives is the rumours themselves:
The legends of Love we share, like sacred bread;
The Hell-accented stories of Beauty and Truth;
The rumours which are only rumours

But are, maybe, enough.

My first photoshoot.

Mum and dad in their courting days.
(He was a wonderful ballroom dancer.)

All of us: from left to right – Mum, Brendan, Gerard, Moya, Declan, me and Dad.

Dad's first shop
in Newcastle –
The Bridge Fish Shop,
beside Mrs Boyle's chippy.

The only photo from our life in the caravan –
Mum on the steps, 1972.

When I was still holy: after being
confirmed by Bishop William
Philbin.

Pagan – the legendary
Patrician Youth Club gig, 1978.

Moya and I beside Dad's new shop, The Sea Shell,
which had just opened. (We lived above the shop.
Note the name of the boutique beside us.)

My brother Brendan

A photo Mum took in the Quad after my
graduation. (I got a 3rd. I told them it was
done in reverse order.)

Receiving an MBE from Prince Charles.
(He asked me if I knew Ted Hughes, who
had just died.)

Left – Jack and Molly (1).

Speaking to groups about poems has been a big part of my life. In this photo by
Maura Johnston I'm speaking to a group of chairs at the end of the school day.

Mum.

Myself and the Boss, at the
Heaney Homeplace.
(Photo: Elaine Forde)

At the home of the President of Ireland, Michael D. Higgins, after reading some of my
poetry.

My wife Bron.

My dog Thomas (RIP), an afficionado of the smokable hydrangea.

Standing outside the Playhouse in Derry, where I worked over the course of a year on a play about the Troubles.

Jack and Molly (2). They'd each made me a birthday cake.

An essay, somewhere

Somewhere in the archives of Belfast Magistrates' Court – unless there's been a redd-out of such things – there is an essay by me on the evils of drink, and a poem.

I hope nobody ever digs them out. They are grim. The road to them included a number of previous stops in court; a scar above my right eye; a sense of shame you could have photographed; and an overdraft as big and obdurate as Donard.

Eventually I came up before a magistrate who wasn't impressed. Charlie Stewart (though I didn't know it then) was regularly in the papers himself on account of his judgements. He'd once bound a dog over to keep the peace, and had also sentenced a member of a leading Belfast folk group to play a benefit for the Simon community, instead of something worse.

Initially I had no lawyer to plead my case before him. I think I was charged with "criminal damage, while out of the skull". I was advised to get a hold of somebody – anybody – as soon as possible, and ended up with a fella who was nearly as young as myself. I remember him asking me very intently before the hearing if, given that this wasn't my first court appearance, there was anything I could think of to say in mitigation. Not even sure of its relevance myself, I mentioned that I'd recently had a poem on the back page of *The Irish Press*. He grasped at this, and ran with it.

"He's a bit of a poet, your honour," was his opening gambit. Mr Stewart fell on this like an unbound dog on a bone. "He's a *what*?", he exploded, and the rest is a blur, to be honest.

The upshot was that he remanded me in custody until his next case, to teach me a lesson. I thought this might mean an hour or two in the "townhall cells" in the same building, but I was mistaken. He had no further cases that day, and no one seemed sure when his next one was.

I was remanded to Crumlin Road Gaol, then filled to the gills with paramilitary prisoners. I will never forget the trip from Chichester Street in the prison bus. I will never forget being told to strip and get into a bath, nor the sights and smells of "The Base", as the remand floor was called. I'll never forget the slopping out (which was still done then), nor the utter indifference – at best – of the prison doctor. Once again, I was living in a film.

I will also never forget the kindness of Michael and Marie (the couple who used to come to our Friday night sessions), who left me in cigarettes - a godsend at the time; nor the words of the Base officer who told me on the morning of my hearing that I may well end up back in the Crum to serve out a sentence. If I did, he said, and I was sent to either the Loyalist or Republican wings, I should keep my nose clean and my mouth shut, for my own good ...

"Good times," as my son would now say, ironically, but not the worst. The worst was when I heard of my brother Brendan's death. As you will hear, I gave the drink up in the end, but poor Brendan couldn't. He tried, I really think he tried, but it carried him off. In the last few years of his life he lived in warden-assisted housing at the bottom of Durham Street in Belfast. I visited him regularly. I had my own key. Sometimes he'd be unconscious, sometimes sober-ish, and occasionally sober. I didn't know what to do.

A psychiatric nurse advised me to pick a time when I thought I could visit him every week, and to turn up each week on the appointed day at the appointed time. If he was conscious, we could talk or go for a coffee; if he was unconscious, I could do the dishes or clean his bathroom (I've never seen a bathroom like it in my life), and leave a note to let him know I'd been.

This is what I did. I went every Tuesday.

He died between Tuesdays.

For Brendan

There's something I meant to say to you
Before you went to sleep.
It was too late in the day,
But it'll keep.

Piercing the fog

Like myself, Brendan's boats were all buoyed up when he started to drink. And like myself, he didn't know it was corroding the bottoms of them. We also shared a vagueness, a kind of protective fog, which must have been annoying to the people who needed us clear-headed. I could sometimes retreat or contract, making myself small, like a creature preparing for winter.

And a brutal winter came when we were told that our mum was dying. I remember being in the consultant's room of the hospital where she was being treated, when the doctor turned on a light-box to show us scans of her vital organs.

"As you can see for yourselves," he said, "it looks like a plum duff".

The shocking nature of what we were being told, and the blatant manner of its telling, shook me out of whatever had me etherised at the time. This was my mum, our mum. She was just in her 50s. She was younger than I am now.

She came home, and my dad was good to her – everyone was good to her. A complete stranger arrived with a fragment of the true cross ("never known to fail"). But neither that, nor Knock, nor a visit to a kind of monk made any difference. And my dad was obliged to source booze again – for the monk.

Mum began to drift in and out of sleep, then in and out of comas. Around the end of November I thought she would never wake again. But when I was visiting on December the 2nd, I heard a noise on the stairs. I rushed out to see mum edging down them in a determined daze (if there is such a thing). She was clutching her handbag, and she looked like her clothes had been thrown at her rather than put on.

"Is it your daddy's birthday?," she asked me, and I had to think. But *she* must have thought of it somewhere inside her coma; and she was right, it was. I tried to urge her back up to bed, where any decent person in her condition should have been, but she was having none of it. She told me that she wanted to get dad a birthday present, and if I wouldn't go into town with her, she'd go on her own.

She was a woman on a mission, several missions in fact. In the course of the next 2 hours she bought dad a wee present; she called on the doctor and chemist to thank them for all they'd done for her – day and night – to give her relief from the pain of her pitiless illness; and she even insisted on taking me for tea and a bun, though her energy was leaving her.

I got her home and walked her up the stairs to her bed. She thanked me for taking her into town, and even managed a smile. She never walked down the stairs again, and died a week later.

I think we'd all say that whatever compassion is in us, whatever bit of selflessness we have, has its source in this woman. I actually don't think she knew how to do a bad turn on anyone. I wish I had known her when I had children myself; I wish that they'd known her, and that she'd known them. I know that it was mum's example which ultimately taught me to leave the cave, pierce the fog, and enter the world as a nett contributor when I could at all. It's through mum's example that I know we belong together as human beings – that the small streams of our lives have a point of confluence somewhere.

Getting to grips with my own isolation, becoming involved in work in Bosnia, Israel-Palestine and other places, has its origin in Marie Gorman (nee Cull) from Dromore, County Down.

The Islandman

From my island to your mainland home
I call across the water that I love you.
This is only wise. Of course I do.
You bring me all the things I cannot grow.

But you call back to say you love me too,
And this defeats me. What is here for you?
Perhaps the winters charm you, for a time?
Or have you re-developments in mind?

For I have not the bravery to know
That you might say it just because it's so.

Srebrenica Haikus

(On July 11 each year – the anniversary of the date on
which the massacre began of well over 8,000 mostly
Bosnian Muslim men and boys – relatives gather for
a funeral for the recently identified. I once heard a
grieving mother say that she was "happy" to be there.)

I am happy today
Because I am able to bury
My son.

I am happy today
To be able to do what needs
To be done.

I am happy today
To welcome the beloved bones of him
Home.

Stop

(In response to the Gaza war of summer 2014)

Today I bury my child
Stop
And it was you who killed my child
Stop
I know that he wasn't the target
Stop
But that doesn't make him any less killed.

I know that "these things have contexts"
Stop
I have walked all around the contexts
Stop
I have tried unfamiliar angles
Stop
And they don't make him any less killed.

You say, "what should we do – tell me?"
Stop
And I say, "don't murder my child"
Stop
"Walk as far away from that as you can"
Stop
"Move forward, away from that thing"
Stop

And you say you are "just like" me
Stop
That we feel and we do the same things
Stop
I know what you mean, but we don't
Stop
For today you don't bury your child

Stop

Stargazing

I read poems at the Commonwealth Literature Festival in Edinburgh in 1986. Margaret Atwood was there, Les Murray, Tony Harrison and many other stars. Among them the lovely Bernard MacLaverty and the lovely Ben Okri. The three of us went out for a drink, and we laughed our legs off.

Finding myself legless, I stayed while they went home. The next thing I remember is walking above Edinburgh as the sun came up. It was a beautiful thing to behold, as was I (like hell). I was in a part of the city I didn't know, but it seemed to be the hilly outskirts. Reaching into my pocket I found there was nothing there: not my wallet, my room key, or the return ticket back to Ireland. I was, as the Bard has it, "the thing itself, unaccommodated man". Which is not a good thing to be early on a Sunday morning. With nothing open, no one contactable, no way home.

That was the last time I was drunk. Through a chance meeting with someone from the Festival, through her kindness, I got back home to Northern Ireland, shaken and stirred. It was confirmed that I was going to be a father, and a strange thing happened. I threw an idea in front of myself, not with deliberation – but idly, like a yawning angler casting. The bizarre thought went something like this: imagine if this wee person who's coming never saw me drunk. Imagine if they never heard me "explaining" where I had been. Imagine if they never saw me flapping at my pockets in panic.

And somehow that idea developed traction, and she never has. Nor has her brother, who arrived five-and-a-half years later. Any father would say it I know, but it's nonetheless true: that my two, Molly and Jack, are the greatest gifts life has given me. I will be in debt to them for as long as I live (hopefully in a literal sense, in later years).

Let me add this for now, and let it be enough. On the nights on which each of them were born, after everything was done, I went off and lay down for a while with my eyes wide open. Not with fear – not even with the first one, Molly – but with wonder. It was as if my eyes were crammed full of stars, and I couldn't shut them.

The light from those stars has never dimmed. It never could.

From
The Skull
Beneath the Skin

Here are the stories I've tried to pass on to my children,
These are the ones that I've told them, since they were small:

That life is mostly good, and mostly long;
That matches cure the darkness at a stroke;
That words are right, and violence is wrong;
That they are loved;
That dreaming is their work;
And that there will always be light up ahead
Because they are so full of light themselves.

These are the stories I've tried to pass on to them both;
These are the ones that I've told, with my heart in my mouth.

For Jack

(On his first day at school)

You're the only person I know
Would kiss me through a cobweb
As you did today, through the bars of the school,
And not bat an eyelid.

You turned away,
With the best part of a cobweb glued to your face
And left me standing, with the rest on mine,
Like a touch of sun
Or the skin of love.

Rockport

(For Molly, on her 18th birthday)

I can see you now
You are no size, on the rocks,
And my head is full
And my heart is in my mouth
As it always is when I talk about you,
Till I stop
Being afraid that you might fall,
And know you must.

So brave clamberer over rocks,
And shedder of light,
May you know how lovely you are
May that hold you up.
Or,
May this world bounce for you when you fall
Like a rapped door.

On the
night that
you were born

On the night that you were born
You were handed straight to me,
Like a special fish that had slipped
From a special sea.

And I held you like a bubble
Upon my fingertips;
I held you like a moment
Made of milk.

And love was a river in me
Sprung with a sudden force,
And you were both its purpose
And its source

For on the night that you were born
A whole world stopped in me;
Then shook, and started over,
Perfectly.

Falling down a well

When I was at primary school a peripatetic music teacher (not Carl Hardebeck) decided that he'd put a bit of a choir together for the craic. Those of us in the room were called upon to sing the national anthem of Newcastle County Down, *The Mountains of Mourne*. I did so with gusto, without fear or restraint, and felt a poke on my shoulder. There are times when I feel that poke on my shoulder still.

"What's your name,?" asked the teacher.

"Gorman sir."

"Well 'Gorman sir', listen to me. I think you'd maybe be better off miming in the corner."

For 35 years now I have worked with people in groups of one sort or another. And many of them seem to have been told, in their lives or by their lives, that they should be miming in a corner. In other words that standing up and telling or singing or dancing or painting their story is not for them. Those are things for other people – particular, special people.

A lot of my work with groups has been about opposing that.

That harsh, that withering inner voice can still speak to me when I'm low –

telling me that I'm a fraud with a moral vacuum at its heart. I can deal with it now (mostly) by agreeing with it, fulsomely, and moving on to something else.

But I'm sure it's been a contributing factor (along with other things mentioned in this book) to the depression and anxiety which have stalked me like bad wee shites.

These days I'm good, but in my early 40s I was not a bit good. I ended up with the GP, and was just in the middle of explaining to him – with great intent and my eyes closed – that I shouldn't really be there at all, when I opened my eyes to find I was blinded by a fall of tears.

I was given anti-depressants for the first time, and I slept a lot. Sometimes it felt like I was falling down, even in bed; but mostly it felt like I had fallen down a well. I could still see a circle of light, and I could hear and be heard. I just didn't seem able to climb up the sides of the thing.

When we were kids, after the family reunited, dad had been in the "Mental". (This is what the Downshire Hospital was called by the locals.) Brendan would later be in the Downshire himself, and I've since heard that mum had also had residential care.

My heart is with people struggling with their mental health and their being. So is my own flawed hand. How could it not be? Here are a couple of poems I have written for people in difficulty.

Acts of Resilience

If you are lost,
If you're out of your depth,
If you cannot explain
Yourself to yourself,

If you're too tired to sleep,
Too tender to touch,
And if even a little
Is much too much,

If the trails to what's sweet
Have all grown cold,
Or you're full of fright
Like a falling child,

Then the thing is to *act*
As brave as you're not -
Act like your life depended on it.

Act like a child
Who is simply free;
Pretend you're as big
As the shadows you see.

Borrow from dreams
That you've had, and you will;
Gather the pieces,
Know you are whole.

A
Time
Comes

And a time comes
When your time comes,
When fear can't stay immense
And takes a chair, like everybody else.

A time comes when you conjure strength
Like water out of air,
A thing you didn't even know
Was there.

A time comes when you find a voice
You find to be your own;
You raise it, like a sail,
And head for home.

A time comes when you know
The bites have healed around your tongue;
A time comes when you know
A time will come.

A Story about a China Doll

The point of this hybrid of selected writings and memoir is that the memoir parts might throw some light on the others. Hopefully they are interesting in themselves, but they're supposed to address the question, "who the hell has done this writing, and why?" And in that context I must tell you a story Granny Cull told me.

Granny Cull (my mother's mother) was a lovely woman with secret stashes of sweets in her pockets. She was also very smiley, and had a wealth of stories about people (as mum had). This is one about herself when she was wee, that she told me when I was.

Lizzie Downey, as she was then, loved school, and she was good at school. But one day she was told that she couldn't go to school any more. Her mother had fallen ill, and she was needed at home. There was a bit of a farm in the family, and her father, older brothers, and occasional farm hands had to be fed. Not to mention that her mother needed looking after. Lizzie was 10. It would turn out to be her mother's final illness, but nobody knew that.

Lizzie went about her hard work with diligence and good humour, and it was noticed. Her father said to her, "Lizzie you're a great girl, and do you know what I'm going to do? The next time the fair's in Dromore I'm going to buy you a doll – a china doll for yourself, for all you've done in the house here".

This was a mighty promise, which the young girl treasured in herself. It got her through difficult weeks, then months, as harvest time came and her mother grew sicker and sicker.

An aunt came to live in the house to help out. Lizzie found the older woman's ways a challenge, but the fair day was up ahead like a promise of sun. And she would soon have a doll, a china doll, of her own.

As her mother took a turn, a final turn, for the worse, the house filled with the comings and goings of other people. The fair day was close, but that was the last thing on anyone's mind. Except for wee Lizzie's, who asked her aunt in a quiet moment one day if she thought there was any chance of the china doll now, given everything.

The aunt drew the back of her hand across Lizzie's face. And there was no mention of a china doll, or any doll, ever again.

I was 5 when she told me that story, and it filled me up. I was incensed at the injustice of the blow, full of sympathy for the wee girl, and beside myself that the promise had not been kept.

It's a small thing, but life is mostly made up of little things. And it strikes me that one of the great tragedies of turbulent times is how the small things – the quieter voices, the personal dreams – lose all of their value, and cannot be heard, in the clamour.

This too, it seems to me, is loss of life.

And that's the idea behind all the work I've done in relation to conflict – that individual stories *matter*, even when the ground is shaking, because we are all individuals; that stories – the details of stories – are connective human tissue.

Here is an essay setting out how I got involved in this sort of work. Followed by a play extract and a recent poem which have resulted from it. There have been many other pieces in this vein. All down, in a way, to a 10-year-old Lizzie Downey.

Glow-Worms

(My chapter of the TUH book, Stories in Conflict)

The only sensible thing for me to do in a book like this is to tell a story. It is also the only thing I am entitled to do. I am not a community relations worker or a mediation expert, I am a writer; a story-teller. This, then, is the story of how I entered the arena of reconciliation work. By the side door, and with nerves you could have photographed.

Like most things with writers, it begins with notions or ideas. Either you believe that everybody's personal story is part of a shared human story, or you don't. I have always believed that, and I have always believed that the things we do or don't do, and the people we are, influence the general health of our communities and our world. In that sense I am part of an overall colour – a colour that is a wee bit brighter or duller, because of me.

"Fair enough," you might think. "Vague enough," might be more to the point. I had a generalised, ungathered set of notions about peace and goodwill. It was as pretty, and about as illuminating, as mist.

Occasionally, of course, that mist lifted, or was pierced. Most of my life has been lived here, in the place of my birth, and I share with everyone who has lived through the time of "the Troubles" the shadow cast across our backs by certain key events. Bloody Sunday; Bloody Friday; Darkley, and the deaths of children. Listening to Gordon Wilson as I made toast the morning after the Enniskillen bombing – *having* to listen to his story because of the note of pure truth in his voice. Not only hearing, but learning something from him. Something I didn't know before – undeniable; prophetic and profoundly anti-death.

And I would ask myself, at such times, "what has all this to do with me? And what have I to do with all this?" I would ask it for a while. And I'd ask myself how peace might come here, and I even thought I knew. I thought it might come like a song that carried all before it. Or that an Ulster Gandhi might emerge whose ideas would light up the horizon like a beacon of hope. But that person didn't seem to come. And the shadows on our backs seemed to thicken. And I half-forgot where I was. And the mist came down again.

And then something happened which got under my skin, and stayed. You can ask me why this particular death did that, but I do not know. There had been so many other deaths – some a lot closer to "home". But this one caught me off guard completely. I was thrown side-ways.

In an awful kind of way you will understand, it was a "mundane" story. I was watching the news across my tea-tray one evening when there was a phone interview with Rev. William McCrea about a relative of his, a part-time soldier, who had been shot dead earlier in the day. Mr McCrea's voice was breaking. When he spoke about the man's son, it broke. He told how the young boy had gone to the phone and rung his granny. "Granny," he'd said, "can you come and mind us? Because a bad man has shot my daddy dead."

This was round about 1990, if I'm not mistaken. Maybe it was because I had a wee one about that age myself; maybe it was Mr McCrea's voice, so unadorned and vulnerable; or maybe it was the idea of a youngster asking a loved one to keep him from harm, when he'd just borne witness to about as much harm as you can imagine. I honestly don't know. But I know that something inside *me* broke, and I determined to connect what I did as a writer with what was happening around me as I wrote.

And I wasn't too sure how to do that. When I think of an image of citizenship, model citizenship, I think of the act of blood donation, for it is easy to trace the thin red line from the act itself to its benefit to other people. Not so with the activity of writing. I have heard it described as everything from "a waste of trees" to "wanking in the margins". Of course it's always meant more than that to *me* but, in the wake of the murder of Mr McCrea's relative, I needed to define its worth in a way I could stand over. I needed to define it in relation to the place where I'd always lived. And if I couldn't, I decided, I'd do something else instead. Something with at least a shred of dignity to it.

In the context of Northern Ireland and its problems, such a personal dilemma was of very little consequence. But it mattered to me, and I defined the dilemma like this: "This is my home. I am a writer. What can I *do*? How can I be a nett contributor to life here in a low, dark time? Does worrying stories into shape have any *value*?"

My first answer was of course it does – it has value *and* resonance. I worked in the theatre, and what happens in a theatre? The lights go down, and something glows in the dark. (Back to the idea of a beacon or bonfire of hope.) So that was my job – helping something to glow in the dark. And if that wasn't a useful job for a Northern Irish person, what was?

The argument made a kind of sense, but I wasn't convinced. It hugged itself a little too much. It was a wee bit up itself.

My second thought was that writers can be useful precisely *because* they stand back from the fray. Rather than approach issues by the Route One of organisations or politics, they take a step back, have a think, and approach those issues side-ways. Not only that but, in writing our stories for the company of *strangers*, we have to think about what might carry to people not like ourselves. So our concern is what resonates across differences and division. We look for, and emphasise, what's common or shared among people.

Again, you would think this is good work for someone from here. And again, though I knew what I meant, I wasn't persuaded by my own line of thinking.

But that was the point – I was relying too much on myself, and, if you feed on only what *you* know, you end up under-nourished. Then it happened again. I was caught out by something I overheard. It was a radio documentary, revisiting a victim of "the Troubles" – a woman whose husband had been shot dead some years previously. (I'm glancing at the sentence I've just written, and realise what I've done. "*Victim of the Troubles*" tells you nothing. It's a flat, "administrative" kind of phrase which wants to redd up reality. But by God this woman and her story weren't to be denied.)

She was angry, and absolutely ready to say her piece. She told us how five years before, on the day of the killing, she had been visited by reporters, most of whom wanted answers to two questions: Have you anything to say to the killers?, and How do you feel?

Looking back, the first question annoyed her because it called her out into a fixed position of public utterance, at the precise moment in her life when she was least fit to go on the record. More for the reporters' sake than anything, she said *something*. Something banal.

But when she spoke about being asked how she felt, there was no decorum. She ripped into the people who'd asked such a lazy, cruel thing. What she wanted to do, most of all, was go back and give an answer along these lines:

"If you want to know how I feel, sit down there and stay till the morning. I'll tell you about my husband: who he was, and who he was to *me*. I'll tell you the whole story – how we met, why I married him, what he thought about things. I'll tell you why I loved him; why the kids loved him; how he made me laugh. And then you might at least *begin* to know the shape of who I've lost. And then you might begin to have an inkling of how I feel!"

That's a true version, if not verbatim report, of what she said. I was wrestling with how I could contribute here. I heard this woman. And then I *knew*. "If you want to know my story, sit down there and stay till the morning." *I* could do that, I thought to myself. That's something I *can* do. For I like listening to people's stories, and always have done. Like all writers I'm nosey about people, curious to a fault. (Years later I sought to emphasise this point at a peace conference, telling people that I was "bi-curious", meaning – or trying to mean – *doubly*-curious. Not for the first time, I didn't know what I was saying.)

That idea – that I mightn't be an "activist" but I could sit and listen to people; listen to their "Troubles" stories, because I wanted to – shaped the next years of my life. I went away and thought how to go about it, and the thoughts seemed to breed. From the idea of story-telling grew the idea of a story-telling *museum*. I wrote a lot of things down, to see what they looked like, and fashioned this bit of writing into an article; an article which was published in local newspapers and magazines in the first week of December, 1994. Here – warts, visions, part-baked ideas and all – is the article as it appeared at the time:

WEAVING THE FUTURE STORY
(Dated November 17, 1994)

Rightly or wrongly I have a sense that we are beginning to "come to" – that Northern Irish people are emerging from paralysis, with the stiffness still in our movements and our hearts.

I have a simple idea that, in gathering ourselves as a community for whatever's ahead, it would be useful to gather the stories of what has been happening to us. Some of these will be hard to listen to, and some hard to tell, but I am suggesting that we begin to gather these across the range, as a way of starting to piece together what has happened to us; as a means towards weaving a better future story.

I have in mind a centre where, under one roof, professional and non-professional storytellers can meet in the building of a narrative of the last twenty-five years which can earn some allegiance from most of us. The artistic equivalent, in a way, of what has to happen politically – ie <u>not</u> the production of a pale inoffensive line to which everyone can give their pale inoffensive disinterest, but a vital, grown-up, accommodating version of our time that we can respect the telling of, feel included by, and feel some authorship of.

To be more specific, I am thinking that this place of witness might be called the <u>Crann</u>. Crann is the Irish word for a tree, and the tree is a symbol of growth and inspiration. It can provide rest or a vantage point. One way or another, it hosts a lot of life.

A visit to the Crann would be an emotional experience, because that is what war is; it would be a personal one, for the same reason. The ingredients of the experience could be something like these:

At the heart of the place could be a library of videotapes – hundreds, if not thousands of stories, gathered with the help of film workshops – in which people tell something of what happened to them from 1969 to the present day. Maybe they fell in love; maybe they were bereaved; maybe they were in jail, or confused, or remote from it all; Maybe they were beaten up; maybe they did very well.

Whatever it is, if people wish to register somewhere, publicly, for the record, an account of what the years of "the Troubles" meant to them, here would be a place to do it. I can't off the top of my head think of anywhere else where such a reservoir of feeling and thought on this subject can be said to exist.

So this tape library could be the still centre of the Crann. The "tour" of the rest of the place might include these elements: firstly a mural – on a lovely, big scale – which covered the whole building, and told our whole history. I know that it sounds impossible, but I have seen it done. In the city of Tlaxcala in Mexico I once visited Desiderio Hernandez Xochitiotzin – a contemporary of the famous muralist Diego Rivera – who has painted the history of his people since the dawn of time. It's a monumental history, and a monumental work – at least as difficult an envisioning of history as would be the "Ulster Mural" – for Mexico, too, has been colonised, traumatised, at war with itself over the centuries. And yet Don Desiderio has pulled it off – an enthralling version of Tlaxcala's story which both Spanish and Indian Mexicans feel included by. It covers the walls of the Palacio de Gobierno in his city. He has worked on it for 36 years, and it still isn't finished. It is a fundamentally generous piece of work.

We have artists who could collaborate on such a project here – who could cover the walls of the Crann with living light, and be honest and wise and vibrant in their painting. Such a work could bloom and heal and fascinate. It could draw people to it like flame. It is not impossible.

Alongside the landscape of the mural could be a soundscape. Not a bland voice giving a history lesson, but a tape inspired by the mural at critical points, and relating to it in creative, unambiguous ways. It might include actuality sound of a depicted event; pieces of music; news reports; relevant ambient sound. It might be launched by the mural into an orbit of its own but it would be clear, and clearly part of the unfolding story.

The telling of that story is not an elitist activity, nor would you need A-levels, or even the 11-Plus to get something out of a visit to the Crann. It would be put in place by people concerned with opening eyes, including their own, and touching hearts. Touch would be very important. I hope that pieces of sculpture might be placed at points of significance or opportunity, to add resonance and extend the overall vision. There should be moments in the tour of the Crann when to reach out and touch a particular piece is to feel a new level of hope, relief or sadness.

The tape room; the mural; the soundscape; the pieces of sculpture – these could be augmented by activities in a small theatre where debates could be held and speeches given; plays or concerts performed. Not tired debates or lazy performances, but open exchanges in which people could give off what often lies beneath the surface – shards of insight, strokes of hurt, bits of confusion or dreaming.

The important thing is to create a space in which as many people as possible feel entitled to respond to what we've all witnessed in recent years – people who are gifted at doing so, and those who need a bit of help. The idea is <u>not</u> to put diverse experiences in a blender and come up with a putty-coloured one which no one ever had, it is the opposite. It is to simply suggest, by housing a wide range of voices and feelings together, that they do exist together, in the one place. And they can do so without destroying the people who have them. We <u>can</u> allow this to happen. It is not impossible.

There is another reason for suggesting the Crann idea. It has to do with what you might call "music". Somewhere in the life of everyone there needs to be <u>freedom</u> – there needs to be a little piece that no one else owns, neither the kids, whom we love; nor the job, which we may not. It is that part of us that sometimes sings for no apparent reason; that acts as the heart's raft; that feels that life's worth living. It is, in a word, morale. And, just as the morale of a person can be worn away, so can the morale of a community. This morale needs nutrients, our hearts need music, especially when they've been so low. And my dream is that the Crann – being welcoming, challenging, unafraid to be visionary – could give a lift to any of us. I admit that it's a dream that is driven by selfishness, but in this sense: I would love to be able to visit such a place myself. We have structured our ways of living nowadays so that the very idea of love is under threat. And yet the cynicism that we wear like winter clothes, I think we have no real fondness for. We, most of us, want to feel we belong. We, most of us, want to feel.

And that will be the work of the Crann – the work of feeling. It will speak to the heart about what the heart can do – the peace it can make, and the hatred it can harbour.

As I said at the outset I feel that we are just "coming round". One image that suggests itself to me is that we have been like people under the knife, but under insufficient anaesthetic to knock us out. We have been dumbly aware of what has been happening to us. We have been screaming silently.

While that image absolves us from too much, you know what I mean. Now is the time to give ourselves voice – to remember, recover, to piece things together. It is in this context that I float the idea of the Crann.

The article ended with an invitation to an open meeting in the Old Museum, Belfast, on December 8th, 1994. I remember having a cup of coffee before that meeting. I spilled some of it on the saucer, on the table and my trousers. I was nervous. I didn't know what I was facing. And I walked in to face ... my da!

I can't tell you how surprised, and touched, I was by his being there. And by the fact that ninety or so other people were there as well. It was a terrific meeting. I had more or less said my piece in the papers, so I spent most of it sitting and listening to other people. When it was over I scribbled in my notebook, "this thing could either be very good, or very bad".

I was mandated by that meeting to go off and put flesh on the bones. I spent the next year or so out and about in all kinds of communities (courtesy of a grant from the Cultural Traditions Group), checking out if there was a welcome for these ideas on the ground. I reported back regularly to further meetings in the Old Museum, and in Derry. That year among people was a real education for me, and put manners on some aspects of the "story-telling museum" idea. I was reminded that being beside people, and *listening* to them, had to be at the heart of it all – listening to their stories until they themselves thought they'd been told.

I also learned that in Northern Ireland story itself can be a kind of weapon. It was as if one community was saying to the other, "our story is *better* than yours. It is richer and warmer". While the retort seemed to be that "*ours* is more steadfast and decent". The stories were ranged against each other – the very telling of them an act of aggression. "Ours blows yours out of the water!", we yelled across a chasm. There is little or no chance of *hearing* amid clamour like that.

Which is not to say that bearing witness can or should be a neutral activity – especially witness dealing with a time of such ferment and hurt. But the Crann was to be about helping people to *hear*, as well as tell, such stories. And if they're just being thrown about like stones, they're very hard to take in.

So that was the challenge – not only to encourage people to tell their own stories of "the Troubles" but to tell them, without compromise, in a way that might be *heard*. I met with many small groups of people, in their own communities, trying to embody the ideas that this Crann thing could be trusted; that the desire to hear their stories – whatever they were – was genuine; and that those stories would not be used against them in any way.

By this stage there were a brave few other people involved. I could mention a lot of names, but there's a couple that I *have* to mention: Maureen Hetherington, then Community Relations Officer with Derry City Council, became Chair of the Crann group, then the formal committee, and contributed greatly; and Maureen Mackin, a business and arts consultant, helped us formulate a three-year development plan. One effect of having good people challenging and extending the original idea was that it became more focussed and distinct, and could be carried more simply. Compare my original, exhausting attempts to corral the elements of vision with these paragraphs from the flyer and Development Plan (1996):

Because Northern Ireland is the way that it is, there is no one who speaks for us all. There is no one who embodies the soul of the place and can tell its true story, for it is a splintered story. We all carry shards of it with us.

It is the purpose of An Crann/The Tree to attempt to piece together the story of "the Troubles" in human terms – the terms of anyone willing to contribute.

In gathering contributions for An Crann/The Tree we will strive to be genuinely inclusive, helpful and sensitive to people who may be relating or re-living hurtful times.

We will consider that we hold all contributions in trust.

This, very briefly, is how the process worked. The flyer carried an invitation to any individual or group interested in recording their experiences of "the Troubles" to get in touch. In other words there was no "cold-calling". One of us (usually me) would then meet with the group so they could see the cut of our gib. And over six or more weeks – two hours per week – we would move towards a telling, and then writing down, of experiences. Often the group would ask me to do the writing, but I never did. I believe in writing, but I believe that it happens in the *arm* – in other words when you put something down on paper you often come up with things that you didn't actually know that you knew, if you see what I mean.

I say that we "moved towards" these stories, and that is crucial. Most of the people I worked with had been deeply affected by "the Troubles", in one way or another. How can you parachute among such people to share stories of conflict when you've no other stories connecting you? For the first couple of sessions we'd talk about everything but. We'd have the craic – we'd talk about men and women, anything – humour was the element. But we all knew we were gathering ourselves to a different kind of telling. No one's arm was ever twisted, obviously, but a space was made. I was there when many people decided to move into that space. It's a cliché, but it was an absolute privilege. An eavesdropping on private truth.

But part of the idea was to make this more widely available. Some people gave their handwritten accounts to the Crann, some of which were later published in the book *Bear in Mind*. These, and other testimonies were the inspiration for a range of public activities including the Elmwood Hall musical concert *ANAM – A Lament for Unlived Life*, which attempted to take up at the point where words leave off. Ultimately the stories were to be housed in a special place of hope. (A beacon again).

We didn't get there – at least not as the Crann – but we got a fair distance. And many of those involved have taken the ideas and language we helped to develop into their work with other bodies (like Towards Understanding and Healing). For myself I spent 1997 and early 1998 as the full-time director of the project, before going to live in France with my family for a number of years. Before I left I facilitated sessions with 161 groups, involving 1,300 people. It's a time I remember with great fondness, although it nearly wrecked me.

This is a very private, personal story I've been telling you here – about one man's circumspect attempts to be involved with change. But I want to end it with a few more general observations – things that I learned, or was taught, that might be some use.

If you know the *detail* of someone's story, it's harder to hate, or want to hurt them. I can say that with confidence, having heard more stories than most. Also, people need time to tell their stories – more time than most TV or newspaper features allow. As Rev. Ruth Patterson once counselled me, "if you're going to understand and respect someone's story, you have to understand and respect their silence first".

That takes effort, but that effort is important. Why is it important? Because we need to know what happened to people here because *we* are people here. Not to attend to the story of the other, to stay semi-detached, can be like saying "the house is burning down next door, but it's nothing to do with me".

Listening's a practice, and it's an elective thing – a choice. We can listen, and go on listening to the stories we know – the ones that we've always known, and hold very near. But we can also learn how to listen to those ones we don't know – the ones that other people might hold dear, beyond our ken. I think that it's a matter of making space for them – making clearances. So we can take them in – *incorporate* them, literally; be made bigger by them.

For me that's where hope lies – in individuals making the effort to do so. I've spoken about bonfires and beacons in this piece, about big lights illuminating the landscape, but maybe that's not the point. Maybe what we need, rather, is thousands of smaller lights – illuminating the whole place like glow-worms. That makes more sense.

I've also mentioned the challenge of trying to glow in the dark. But things are better and brighter now, and the challenge could develop. How might Northern Irish people shine in more normal times? Glowing in the dark is one thing; learning how to glow in the *light* could be mighty.

From
Loved Ones

(Having being interviewed, earlier in the day, for a book about people bereaved in the Troubles, Bronwen Donnelly wishes she could do it all again, now that it's straight in her mind. She does so, late in the day, on her own. Here she reflects on the day that her son Mark was killed.)

BRONWEN

... Since I was a very little girl, I've carried this nightmare that someday a monster would come. We would all be doing our usual things when, suddenly, it would loom over us as an evil we couldn't see round, it would shatter the day like glass, it would splinter my world. And that is exactly what happened the day that Mark died.

He was up before me that morning, and he'd made the breakfast. Tommy was away with the club, so Mark had the car. He badgered me and badgered me to sit down and eat something with him. But I'm picky in the mornings, and anyway I wasn't in good form. I'd put on an overnight wash and it hadn't come on. In the end he said, "right, that's the last cup of tea I'll make you ..."

Then it happened, in the way that I'd always feared it would. The world blew up in my face – in my dear son's face. I've a memory that doesn't make sense that, just before it happened, I knew it was going to, and I started to run to him.

Gets up.

But that couldn't be right, I came to lying just about here. Like a person who'd been bathing in glass. I was *swimming* in glass and blood and, and I knew that – whatever it meant – my lovely boy was dead.

Now I didn't feel numb, or detached or afraid – not then. I went out to him *(looks out the window)* I went out to him like a prayer. I cradled him *(hugs herself)*, and told him that I loved him very much. I told him in a way I'd never told anyone before. I told him not with love but *as* love, if you see what I mean. I told him in a way that I honestly think might have reached him.

My heart broke then, and my heart is broken now. I'll be heart-broken till they put me in beside him.

Sits down again, and takes another sip of Norfolk Punch.

The next few days, before the funeral, were very hard on me. I was saying to that fella today that I felt really guilty. It was as if I had left Mark, walked out on him for good. We'd become separated – me and my son – forever. And it was my fault, somehow it was my fault. It had to be.

And I was scared, I was so very scared – but I didn't want to be sedated. I knew it was only me could see Tommy through. And I didn't want to be put out on my own account. I didn't want to be evicted from my own mind.

Noeleen knew that I was frightened, and that I didn't want to take anything. But the night before the funeral she asked me to speak to a friend of hers. At least I think he was a friend – she certainly had a lot of time for him. He was the chaplain to one of the universities – I can't remember which.

I told him how I was feeling – so guilty, and so very scared. But he said it was alright to be scared, although it mightn't feel it. He told me that fear could be healing, in its own way. "I often point out to people," he said, "how close the word 'scared' is to 'sacred ' ". I thanked him, but, there again, I didn't mean it.

But I have to say people were kind – that's one thing about this place: we gather round grieving people like straw around eggs. But it's tiring too. Everybody wants to see *you*. And there's only so much sympathy you can take.

I remember that week before the funeral very clearly. I talked to more people in 5 days than in the whole of my life. When they left every night I used to feel that I had done something hard really well. I had come through, endured, acquitted myself with honours, but now it was time to go home – I'd a *need* to go home. Except that's where I was, and that's where the whole thing had happened. I was sorry that I couldn't come and go from the house, like work.

And do you know what was the very hardest thing to bear? The thought that I was nobody's mother any more – no body's. And it's true, I'm not, I'm nobody's mother now. I remember sitting in the church at his funeral thinking, "I'm a mother without children – a stupid, stupid thing. That's what I am: a stupid, stupid thing..."

Field Notes

(50 short lines, 50 years since the start of the 'Troubles')

"Out beyond ideas of wrongdoing and rightdoing there is a field.
I'll meet you there." RUMI

What could make a difference?
What would matter a damn?
What could change the course of us
In the long run?

What have we put in the way of rolling
Once more over the cliff?
What have we never tried,
Or never enough?

What could heal our politics?
What could ring the bells?
Bring us to the table as more
Than furniture ourselves?

I am trying to avoid the word love
As something much too vague.
I am trying to avoid the word love
Like the plague.

What could take us to that place
Where grief is like the sea
To ask if there is anything
We can do?

What could bring us to those people
Hungering for right
To listen to their stories
Through the night?

What could place us near to someone
Driven from their mind
By hurt or fear, in order
To be kind?

I am trying to avoid the word love
So as not to be laughed out of sight.
I am trying to avoid that word
With all my might.

What could make us leave the tracks
That are already laid
And pin us down, like things
Already said?

I am trying to avoid the word love
Like a fully-loaded trap.
I am trying to avoid the word love,
But why would you do that?

For love is thought which has a bit of thought;
Is feeling with an inkling what to do;
Is something in us knows, within its heart,
That there are hearts in other people too.
It stands for something clearly, like a whinbush on the road
Beautifully resolute and gold.
And is the fulsome, real love – love *enough* –
Could keep us going when the going's tough:

A love that is magnificent, or mild;
Love like Solomon's, reaching for the child...

At the very edge of the world there are grounds for hope

It is a fact that in the darkest spaces I have ever been I have eventually found slivers of light, or the ingredients of light.

When we redd out Brendan's flat it was chaos, a tip. But buried under everything I found something no one had expected. A pile, a neat little pile, of correspondence. There were letters from me, but also correspondence concerning his subscriptions to 2 charities – which he had kept up over the years, despite his life being on fire. There were also "riding for the disabled" Christmas cards which he'd bought in advance. These are what I sent out to family the following Christmas.

As a writer I have worked with people hurt by violence for half my life. Most recently with Richard, Victor, Hazel, Tom, Siobhan and Susan – 6 people shaken to the core by the Troubles at home. I worked with them for almost a year. I have never laughed as much in my life as I did in those 12 months. In *Anything Can Happen* the Caretaker, the one made-up character, refers to this laughter at the very end. His are the play's last words.

I told you a poem earlier – *Human Threads* – about the junta in Chile. One of the many people killed during that convulsive time was Victor Jara – a much-loved folk singer, who was lifted in the first days of the coup. Like many others he was taken to the national stadium for questioning and torture. An army captain recognised him, and told his soldiers that he had special plans for Jara. His hands were broken in an attempt to kill his music, but the attempt was unsuccessful.

With broken hands he could no longer play guitar, but he composed and sung out his final song before he was killed. It was taken down by a fellow prisoner, a teacher, who was able to write music.

Even in the face of death I've found that certain things are possible. I told you about my mother rising out of a coma earlier on. A year-and-a-half ago I fell ill myself, with symptoms that seemed like the harbingers of no good thing. In the period that I was wading through tests and results it occurred to me that I might have to have a conversation with my children – a difficult conversation I wasn't looking forward to. I began to think about how I might have it in a way that wouldn't wreck them. Not so that they could ever remember it fondly, but that they'd be able to at all.

In the end I didn't have to have that conversation, thank God. But the feelings had washed through me anyway and, as I do, I wrote a poem. In the poem I found something useful, something good. Something I did not know before I chanced my arm, and wrote it.

And this is the thing about writing – about all the arts – that they make spaces for us; they give us somewhere to go. Hopelessness is when you're up against the wall so tight that there's no light, and it seems that the only way forward is to push your flesh through brick. Art – storytelling, comedy and poetry and music and dancing; painting and acting and sculpture and general mayhem – can alter your stance at the wall, even the wall itself.

At least that's my story, so far. And I'm sticking to it.

The last words of Anything can happen

CARETAKER

... You know I heard them all laughing this morning, and it really threw me. "What have *they* to be laughing about?", I wondered – anyone would. But now I'm thinking to myself that ... maybe you can't cry forever. You can't cry forever, like you can't hold your breath forever – even if you wanted to, even if you tried your best. Your own lungs would fight you for dear life.

And they would win ...

A
Bird

(In memory of Victor Jara)

A bird can sing
With broken wings,
Or none at all.

All that it needs
Is a full throat,
And a hearing;

All it needs
 Is not to be too afraid
Of singing;

All that it needs
Is to be – or have been -
A bird.

On throwing my kids in the air, and letting go

The fondest weight I've known in my life
Is the weight of you two plummeting to earth,
Each of you gathered in, like my whole wealth,
Having eclipsed the sun with your whole self.

And that weight, that lovely weight, that winking flight
Is as dear to me as anything, and as right
As any thing in the painful world is wrong -
Nothing takes a feather from its wing

Not even the thought which, like a cat appears
At odd hours of the night, on silent paws,
That one day the man who plucked you from the air,
That I – in the way of things - will not be there.

And with all my heart, I want you to make peace
With that thought, in your own way, and with this:
That when it's your turn, you should fling me high
Knowing, as I did, it will be ok.

So when it's my time for going, let me go.
Let your grief be just a brief eclipse
For I'll keep going – across the universe -
Telling the stories of you two and me,
Of us.

Postscript

I want to give my dad the last word in this book, in a manner of speaking.

As I said earlier, he hated mum shopping in the covered market when we were kids. Why? Because I think he thought it let us down, or *him* down, that she did. That made no sense to the rest of us, then or now, but it was true that we were falling fast – at least in terms of money and standing.

One day mum bought a cassette recorder in the market – a hefty, old-style black one, the size of a shoe-box. She brought it home with her from work, and it's the first time I ever remember falling in love with a *thing*.

That evening we all clambered over it like a tribe of meerkats. We shouted into it, sang into it, and heard our own voices with glee. It was a magical thing, and we went to bed that night touched by its wonder. Leaving dad in the corner of the living room, mute and inscrutable. He was ill at the time, and he hardly left his chair.

Unusually, the following morning I was up before him. I think it was excitement for the tape recorder had wakened me up. I turned it on, and I heard something which stopped me in my tracks – dad's voice, without its armour or its threat. It was by turns unsure, approachable, even playful. He must have made the recording in the night when he was on his own.

I wish I had taken the cassette out that minute and kept it. I wish I had it now. I wish I'd heard more of that voice when I was growing up – that we all had. But it was in him, it was definitely in him. Something just held it there.

Or maybe you just didn't talk then, as I do now. And maybe that hurt him – his tongue like a fish out of water. I'll never know now, and that's alright.

I love you dad.

Acknowledgements

I would like to thank editors at the following places for commissioning some of the pieces in this book, or work of which those pieces were a part: BBC Radio 3; BBC Network Features; BBC Worldwide; Channel 4 Television; DBA Television; 4 x 4 (Poetry NI); Fallen Angels Theatre Company; The Lyric Theatre, Belfast; OMAC (now the MAC); The Poetry Jukebox; The Resilience Project; The Rian International Immigrant Centre (Boston, USA); The Theatre Peacebuilding Academy; and World Baby Day (in particular, Anna Newell). Thanks also to Eamonn and Maureen at Towards Understanding and Healing, and the Stitched Voices project of Aberystwyth University's International Politics Department. Thanks to Eugene and Sian for their artistic druidery, and to Richie for all his help.

Thank you to the Arts Council of Northern Ireland for their generous support, and a personal thanks to Damian Smyth for his friendship and encouragement down the years.

I have dedicated this book "to my loved ones", and I cannot thank them enough.

Finally – and very importantly – thank you to the people who let me include poems written for them. Loved ones all.

Go raibh míle maith agaibh go léir.

Thank you all very much.